THE HIGHLIGHTED BIBLE

(Book of Psalm Edition)

PATRICIA K. LEWIS

ISBN 978-1-105-60855-1

Then they that feared the LORD spake often one to another: and the LORD hearkened, and heard it, and a book of remembrance was written before him for them that feared the LORD, and that thought upon his name. *Malachi 3:16*

DEDICATION

I dedicate this book to the Holy Spirit, the third person of the Trinity. When I think about you, and all that you are, two words always describe my present thoughts about you – "with me". Your presence as a comforter and one who leads and guides me into all truth has made my life so very real. This is why "reality" has taken on a whole new meaning in my life. Thanks to you, my friend.

CONTENTS

PREFACE

INTRODUCTION

PART I

How to Stand in the Light You Have Received

PART II

The Highlighted Word of God in Jesus

PART III

Top Highlighted Scriptures from the Book of Psalm

PART IV

Bible Versions & Translations

PREFACE

The Highlighted Bible is a book about you, your bible, and solutions you create as a result of your study habits. This book was developed to ignite static bible study notes into a dynamic blaze of God's word in action. The primary objective of the Highlighted Bible is to bring to your attention how important your bible has become after repeated use in the study of God's word.

ABOUT YOU

You attend church a lot. You hear sermon after sermon, sit through bible study weekly, and you do even more by attending special events to help deepen your understanding of God's word. You may border on addiction because you consume enormous amounts of bible-based information every chance you get. After a period of time, you have racked up hundreds of hours of hearing bible-based messages.

ABOUT YOUR BIBLE

If you follow along during sermons, studies, or lessons, you may have made a note, annotation, or highlight here or there within the pages of your bible, or inside a notebook. During this time, you make sure everything is recorded correctly because you are a perfectionist. This is the creative process that produces your highlighted bible. Just flip through the pages and realize your time investment.

RESULTS

All truths are easy to understand once they are discovered; the point is to discover them. — Galileo Galilei

The Highlighted Bible is a record book! When you flip through your bible and find evidence of the sermon from last week, the message from this past Easter, or the series of sermons from the last revival meeting – you have discovered truth that can be used today! You must know that you possess a degree of competence that allows you to apply familiar scripture in difficult situations. You demonstrate this competence when you solve a current problem with the understanding of scripture from your highlighted bible. Because of your commitment, you have the ability to produce bible-based information (God's word) to answer questions and solve problems.

INTRODUCTION

Do you own a bible?

I believe I own about twenty-five and one-half. Well, it sure looks like half of one is missing! The bible I use most often is a King James Version I have owned for fifteen years or more. To the untrained eye (namely my husband) it may appear to be ripe for the recycle bin. The leather cover is extremely worn and it is covered with stains from misuse. It is likely that I have used it as a drink coaster, or a fly swatter, or as some other product-substitute because it is always near and handy.

Inside my bible, many pages are littered with highlighting, annotations, links to other passages, song lyrics, e-mail addresses, dates and phone numbers. But what really stands out is that when I thumb through the entire book, I see what must be years of sermon text, bible study lessons, personal study notes, and notations from many other events – all chronicled into a record that strikes me as being amazing.

With such particularity, various scriptures are highlighted or underscored. Cross-references are annotated in the columns. Hebrew or Greek words are defined. Interpretation of a word or text is penned inside the available spaces between verses. A note reminding me to "check this out in the Amplified" stands out on the page because it is marked with at least three stars. So much time and care is poured into making my bible something more, something greater, something I can believe in.

What happened here is that I had created a journal that outlines my Christian walk. And as I look closer, I see a pattern of observable behaviors demonstrated when I encountered difficult life events. For instance, I gave one hundred dollars to a friend who had fallen on hard times due to no fault of her own. But as I recall, I too was only one week from being penniless (but this was my fault entirely). The inspiration for my actions came from Matthew 9:36. I believe that I received this scripture text during a bible study approximately one year earlier. This scripture prompted me to show compassion and respond accordingly to meet the need of a friend and not just sit around and feel sorry for her.

Another time, years after helping my friend, I remember being unsure how I should respond (if at all) to the cry of help from thousands of homeless victims after hurricane Katrina devastated the Gulf Coast. At this time I was in law school and my family's resources were budgeted. Once again, after thumbing through my bible, I came across Matthew 9:36 and after a short discussion with my husband, we made a contribution corporately and individually that really made a difference in the lives of families affected by the catastrophe.

Your highlighted bible is a dynamic resource created over a period of time. It holds evidence of sermons, studies, classes, seminars, camp meetings, revivals, and workshops you recorded. You have created something so very unique and valuable because of your time and study spent in God's word. Here is why I am excited about this book; it is designed to help you focus on the answers you have already received from God. These answers can be found today, inside your highlighted bible.

PART I

How to Stand In the Light You Have Received

But as for you, continue to hold to the things that you have learned and of which you are convinced, knowing from whom you learned [them], 2 Timothy 3:14 Amplified Bible

"The word is a lamp unto my feet", Psalm 119:105

Learning, for many, is the lifelong process of transforming information and knowledge into observable behaviors, skills, and attitudes. Take, for example, when you volunteer to assist Habitat for Humanity, or contribute to the United Way, or act as a lay-away angel – you clearly demonstrate a superior level of learning in the area of compassion. Your contribution to humanity shines bright and the lesson of compassion is alive and active in the earth!

A demonstration of compassion is an innate behavior and a conditioned response to a cry for help. When you allow God's word to enter your heart, it directs your feet, your actions, and your desire. God illuminates or highlights his word in your heart so that your response will be the right one to meet the present need.

The very first step you must take in learning how to stand in the light you have received is to "focus on the highlights".

Take a few minutes and look at your personal bible and notes. Don't be concerned if the highlights or notes are few in number. What matters is that you have proved you are willing to learn important lessons. That's why it is easy for you to sit through hours of sermons, teachings, and lectures. What you get in return is a treasure trove of benefits, gifts, and miracles ready to spring into action whenever you act on the highlighted word you know and understand.

Next, when difficult situations arrive, don't let them overtake you. Instead, speak what God has said about this situation! "By his stripes, I am healed"! "I can do all things through Christ who strengthens me"! "The joy of the Lord is my strength"! Be a doer of the word of God – this is a major part of standing in the light you have received.

Finally, you must give thanks. Gratitude hastens the arrival of your answer. As always, your answer arrived the moment you believed. Giving thanks to God while you are experiencing difficult times demonstrates that the highlighted word in your bible is actually living inside of you. Your thanks and praise to God proves that you are standing in the light you have received.

PART II

The Highlighted Word of God in Jesus

Matthew 4:4

But he answered and said, It is written, Man shall not live by bread alone, but by every word that proceedeth out of the mouth of God.

DO AS JESUS DID

Jesus' response to Satan is a great example to follow. His demonstration of knowledge in the law was short, clear, and easy to remember. Undoubtedly, Jesus was extremely knowledgeable in the word of God. His insight into the scriptures was demonstrated as early as age twelve. During his time, he not only mastered the scriptures, but he applied his knowledge of the law in everyday situations.

Jesus' example teaches us how we are to live victoriously and rise above problems. The primary lesson to learn here is "SOLVE PROBLEMS WITH WORD". When things go wrong, don't hesitate to seek out, select, and use the mountain of Word you have noted in your highlighted bible.

The New Testament book of Matthew records about thirty-eight times Jesus referred to scripture:

SCRIPTURE JESUS QUOTED

Matthew 4:4

Jesus quotes Deuteronomy 8:3 in response to Satan's temptation

But he answered and said, It is written, Man shall not live by bread alone, but by every word that proceedeth out of the mouth of God.

Deuteronomy 8:3

And he humbled thee, and suffered thee to hunger, and fed thee with manna, which thou knewest not, neither did thy fathers know; that he might make thee know that man doth not live by bread only, but by every word that proceedeth out of the mouth of the LORD doth man live

Matthew 4:7

Jesus quotes Deuteronomy 6:16

Jesus said unto him, It is written again, Thou shalt not tempt the Lord thy God.

Deuteronomy 6:16

Ye shall not tempt the LORD your God, as ye tempted him in Massah.

Matthew 4:10

Jesus quotes Deuteronomy 6:13

Then saith Jesus unto him, Get thee hence, Satan: for it is written, Thou shalt worship the Lord thy God, and him only shalt thou serve.

Deuteronomy 6:13

Thou shalt fear the LORD thy God, and serve him, and shalt swear by his name.

Matthew 5:17-19

Jesus says He did not come to destroy the Law or the Prophets, but to fulfill. He confirms their inerrancy by saying that not "one jot or one tittle" would pass away till all was fulfilled.

17Think not that I am come to destroy the law, or the prophets: I am not come to destroy, but to fulfil.

18For verily I say unto you, Till heaven and earth pass, one jot or one tittle shall in no wise pass from the law, till all be fulfilled.

19Whosoever therefore shall break one of these least commandments, and shall teach men so, he shall be called the least in the kingdom of heaven: but whosoever shall do and teach them, the same shall be called great in the kingdom of heaven.

Matthew 5:21

Jesus quotes Exodus 20:13 or Deuteronomy 5:17

Ye have heard that it was said of them of old time, Thou shalt not kill; and whosoever shall kill shall be in danger of the judgment:

Deuteronomy 5:17

Thou shalt not kill.

Exodus 20:13

Thou shalt not kill.

Matthew 5:27

Jesus quotes Exodus 20:14 or Deuteronomy 5:18

Ye have heard that it was said by them of old time, Thou shalt not commit adultery:

Exodus 20:14

Thou shalt not commit adultery.

Deuteronomy 5:18

Neither shalt thou commit adultery.

Matthew 5:38

Jesus quotes Exodus 21:24, Leviticus 24:20, or Deuteronomy 19:21

Ye have heard that it hath been said, An eye for an eye, and a tooth for a tooth:

Exodus 21:24

Eye for eye, tooth for tooth, hand for hand, foot for foot,

Leviticus 24:20

Breach for breach, eye for eye, tooth for tooth: as he hath caused a blemish in a man, so shall it be done to him again.

Deuteronomy 19:21

And thine eye shall not pity; but life shall go for life, eye for eye, tooth for tooth, hand for hand, foot for foot

Matthew 5:43

Jesus refers to Leviticus 19:18

Ye have heard that it hath been said, Thou shalt love thy neighbour, and hate thine enemy.

Leviticus 19:18

Thou shalt not avenge, nor bear any grudge against the children of thy people, but thou shalt love thy neighbour as thyself: I am the LORD.

Matthew 6:29

Jesus refers to 'Solomon in all his glory,' a historical reference to I Kings

And yet I say unto you, That even Solomon in all his glory was not arrayed like one of these.

Matthew 7:12

Jesus sums up the Law and the Prophets with the golden rule

Therefore all things whatsoever ye would that men should do to you, do ye even so to them: for this is the law and the prophets.

Matthew 8:11

Jesus makes historical reference to Abraham, Isaac, and Jacob (told of in Genesis), referring to future events in which they will be involved.

And I say unto you, That many shall come from the east and west, and shall sit down with Abraham, and Isaac, and Jacob, in the kingdom of heaven.

Matthew. 8:20

Jesus refers to Himself as the 'Son of Man,' a clear Messianic reference to Daniel 7:13. By calling Himself by this title, Jesus was claiming to be the fulfillment of Daniel's prophecy, the Messiah and the King of 'all peoples, nations, and languages.'

And Jesus saith unto him, The foxes have holes, and the birds of the air have nests; but the Son of man hath not where to lay his head.

Matthew 9:13

Jesus quotes Hosea 6:6

But go ye and learn what that meaneth, I will have mercy, and not sacrifice: for I am not come to call the righteous, but sinners to repentance.

Hosea 6:6

For I desired mercy, and not sacrifice; and the knowledge of God more than burnt offerings.

Matthew 10:15

Jesus speaks of literal, future events involving Sodom and Gomorrah (specifically, the day of judgment). The story of Sodom and Gomorrah is from Genesis, and this saying of Jesus is proof that the Genesis account is literally and historically true.

Verily I say unto you, It shall be more tolerable for the land of Sodom and Gomorrha in the day of judgment, than for that city.

Matthew 10:35, 36

Jesus quotes Micah 7:6

35For I am come to set a man at variance against his father, and the daughter against her mother, and the daughter in law against her mother in law.

36And a man's foes shall be they of his own household.

Micah 7:6

For the son dishonoureth the father, the daughter riseth up against her mother, the daughter in law against her mother in law; a man's enemies are the men of his own house

Matthew 11:10

Jesus quotes Malachi 3:1

For this is he, of whom it is written, Behold, I send my messenger before thy face, which shall prepare thy way before thee.

Malachi 3:1

Behold, I will send my messenger, and he shall prepare the way before me: and the LORD, whom ye seek, shall suddenly come to his temple, even the messenger of the covenant, whom ye delight in: behold, he shall come, saith the LORD of hosts.

Matthew 11:21

Jesus makes reference to past and future events involving Tyre and Sidon (references to which are found in multiple books in the

Old Testament)

Woe unto thee, Chorazin! woe unto thee, Bethsaida! for if the mighty works, which were done in you, had been done in Tyre and Sidon, they would have repented long ago in sackcloth and ashes.

Matthew 12:3-5

Jesus refers to the story of David eating the showbread found in I Samuel 21

3But he said unto them, Have ye not read what David did, when he was an hungred, and they that were with him;

4How he entered into the house of God, and did eat the shewbread, which was not lawful for him to eat, neither for them which were with him, but only for the priests?

5Or have ye not read in the law, how that on the sabbath days the priests in the temple profane the sabbath, and are blameless?

Matthew 12:7

Jesus again quotes Hosea 6:6

But if ye had known what this meaneth, I will have mercy, and not sacrifice, ye would not have condemned the guiltless.

Hosea 6:6

For I desired mercy, and not sacrifice; and the knowledge of God more than burnt offerings.

Matthew 12:29

Jesus refers to the prophet Jonah and the historical city of Nineveh

Or else how can one enter into a strong man's house, and spoil his goods, except he first bind the strong man? and then he will spoil his house.

Matthew 12:42

Jesus refers to the Queen of the South visiting Solomon, an event recorded in I Kings 10

The queen of the south shall rise up in the judgment with this generation, and shall condemn it: for she came from the uttermost parts of the earth to hear the wisdom of Solomon; and, behold, a greater than Solomon is here.

Matthew 13:14

Jesus calls Isaiah 6:9, 10 'prophecy' and quotes it.

And in them is fulfilled the prophecy of Esaias, which saith, By hearing ye shall hear, and shall not understand; and seeing ye shall see, and shall not perceive:

Isaiah 6:9-10

9And he said, Go, and tell this people, Hear ye indeed, but understand not; and see ye indeed, but perceive not.

10Make the heart of this people fat, and make their ears heavy, and shut their eyes; lest they see with their eyes, and hear with their ears, and understand with their heart, and convert, and be healed.

Matthew 15:3-6

Jesus quotes Exodus 20:12, Deuteronomy 5:16, or Exodus 21:17 to rebuke the Pharisees, and He says that those passages are the 'commandment of God.'

3But he answered and said unto them, Why do ye also transgress the commandment of God by your tradition?

4For God commanded, saying, Honour thy father and mother: and, He that curseth father or mother, let him die the death.

5But ye say, Whosoever shall say to his father or his mother, It is a gift, by whatsoever thou mightest be profited by me;

[6]And honour not his father or his mother, he shall be free. Thus have ye made the commandment of God of none effect by your tradition.

Exodus 20:12

Honour thy father and thy mother: that thy days may be long upon the land which the LORD thy God giveth thee

Deuteronomy 5:16

Honour thy father and thy mother, as the LORD thy God hath commanded thee; that thy days may be prolonged, and that it may go well with thee, in the land which the LORD thy God giveth thee.

Exodus 21:17

And he that curseth his father, or his mother, shall surely be put to death

Matthew 15:7-9

Jesus quotes Isaiah 29:13

7Ye hypocrites, well did Esaias prophesy of you, saying,

8This people draweth nigh unto me with their mouth, and honoureth me with their lips; but their heart is far from me.

9But in vain they do worship me, teaching for doctrines the commandments of men.

Isaiah 29:13

Wherefore the Lord said, Forasmuch as this people draw near me with their mouth, and with their lips do honour me, but have removed their heart far from me, and their fear toward me is taught by the precept of men:

Matthew 16:4

Jesus again refers to the sign of the prophet Jonah

A wicked and adulterous generation seeketh after a sign; and there shall no sign be given unto it, but the sign of the prophet Jonas. And he left them, and departed.

Matthew 18:16

Jesus quotes Deuteronomy 19:15 to establish doctrine of church behavior

But if he will not hear thee, then take with thee one or two more, that in the mouth of two or three witnesses every word may be established.

Deuteronomy 19:15

One witness shall not rise up against a man for any iniquity, or for any sin, in any sin that he sinneth: at the mouth of two witnesses, or at the mouth of three witnesses, shall the matter be established.

Matthew 19:4-6

Jesus quotes Genesis 1:27, 5:2, and 2:24. He refers to the literal details of the creation account of Adam and Eve to establish the doctrine of marriage.

[4]And he answered and said unto them, Have ye not read, that he which made them at the beginning made them male and female,

[5]And said, For this cause shall a man leave father and mother, and shall cleave to his wife: and they twain shall be one flesh?

[6]Wherefore they are no more twain, but one flesh. What therefore God hath joined together, let not man put asunder.

Genesis 1:27

So God created man in his own image, in the image of God created he him; male and female created he them.

Genesis 5:2

Male and female created he them; and blessed them, and called their name Adam, in the day when they were created.

Genesis 2:24

Therefore shall a man leave his father and his mother, and shall cleave unto his wife: and they shall be one flesh.

Matthew 19:18, 19

Jesus quotes parts of Exodus 20:12-16, Deuteronomy 5:16-20, and Leviticus 19:18

18He saith unto him, Which? Jesus said, Thou shalt do no murder, Thou shalt not commit adultery, Thou shalt not steal, Thou shalt not bear false witness,

19Honour thy father and thy mother: and, Thou shalt love thy neighbour as thyself.

Matthew 21:13

Jesus quotes Isaiah 56:7 and Jeremiah 7:11 in one sentence

And said unto them, It is written, My house shall be called the house of prayer; but ye have made it a den of thieves.

Isaiah 56:7

Even them will I bring to my holy mountain, and make them joyful in my house of prayer: their burnt offerings and their sacrifices shall be accepted upon mine altar; for mine house shall be called an house of prayer for all people.

Jeremiah 7:11

Is this house, which is called by my name, become a den of robbers in your eyes? Behold, even I have seen it, saith the LORD.

Matthew 21:16

Jesus quotes Psalm 8:2

And said unto him, Hearest thou what these say? And Jesus saith unto them, Yea; have ye never read, Out of the mouth of babes and sucklings thou hast perfected praise?

Psalm 8:2

Out of the mouth of babes and sucklings hast thou ordained strength because of thine enemies, that thou mightest still the enemy and the avenger.

Matthew 21:42

Jesus quotes Psalm 118:22, 23

Jesus saith unto them, Did ye never read in the scriptures, The stone which the builders rejected, the same is become the head of the corner: this is the Lord's doing, and it is marvellous in our eyes?

Psalm 118: 22, 23

22 The stone which the builders refused is become the head stone of the corner.

23 This is the LORD's doing; it is marvellous in our eyes.

Matthew 22:31, 32

Jesus quotes Exodus 3:6, 15 and says that these passages were 'spoken to you by God.' This is a direct and unequivocal statement by the Lord Jesus Himself that the words of Scripture, penned by a human being, are in fact the words of God.

31But as touching the resurrection of the dead, have ye not read that which was spoken unto you by God, saying,

32I am the God of Abraham, and the God of Isaac, and the God of Jacob? God is not the God of the dead, but of the living.

Exodus 3:6, 15

6Moreover he said, I am the God of thy father, the God of Abraham, the God of Isaac, and the God of Jacob. And Moses hid his face; for he was afraid to look upon God.

15And God said moreover unto Moses, Thus shalt thou say unto the children of Israel, the LORD God of your fathers, the God of Abraham, the God of Isaac, and the God of Jacob, hath sent me unto you: this is my name for ever, and this is my memorial unto all generations.

Matthew 22:37

Jesus quotes Deuteronomy 6:5, the first and great commandment

Jesus said unto him, Thou shalt love the Lord thy God with all thy heart, and with all thy soul, and with all thy mind.

Deuteronomy 6:5

And thou shalt love the LORD thy God with all thine heart, and with all thy soul, and with all thy might.

Matthew 22:39

Jesus quotes Leviticus 19:18, the second great commandment

And the second is like unto it, Thou shalt love thy neighbour as thyself.

Leviticus 19:18

Thou shalt not avenge, nor bear any grudge against the children of thy people, but thou shalt love thy neighbour as thyself: I am the LORD.

Matthew 22:43-45

Jesus quotes and refers to Psalm 110:1

43He saith unto them, How then doth David in spirit call him Lord, saying,

44The LORD said unto my Lord, Sit thou on my right hand, till I make thine enemies thy footstool?

45If David then call him Lord, how is he his son?

Psalm 110:1

The LORD said unto my Lord, Sit thou at my right hand, until I make thine enemies thy footstool

Matthew 23:39

Jesus quotes Psalm 118:26

For I say unto you, Ye shall not see me henceforth, till ye shall say, Blessed is he that cometh in the name of the Lord.

Psalm 118:26

Blessed be he that cometh in the name of the LORD: we have blessed you out of the house of the LORD.

Matthew 24:15

Jesus quotes Daniel 11:31 and 12:11, speaking of 'Daniel the prophet'

When ye therefore shall see the abomination of desolation, spoken of by Daniel the prophet, stand in the holy place, (whoso readeth, let him understand:)

Daniel 11:31

And arms shall stand on his part, and they shall pollute the sanctuary of strength, and shall take away the daily sacrifice, and they shall place the abomination that maketh desolate.

Daniel 12:11

And from the time that the daily sacrifice shall be taken away, and the abomination that maketh desolate set up, there shall be a thousand two hundred and ninety days.

Matthew 26:31

Jesus quotes Zechariah 13:7, a Messianic prophecy

Then saith Jesus unto them, All ye shall be offended because of me this night: for it is written, I will smite the shepherd, and the sheep of the flock shall be scattered abroad.

Zechariah 13:7

Awake, O sword, against my shepherd, and against the man that is my fellow, saith the LORD of hosts: smite the shepherd, and the sheep shall be scattered: and I will turn mine hand upon the little ones.

PART III

Top Highlighted Scriptures from the Book of Psalm

The Book of Psalm is a common bond that runs deep in the hearts of the church. Psalms is one of the most beloved books of the bible. From a sample of 5500 people that attend church or church events, the following passages were commonly highlighted in personal bibles after being introduced via a sermon, bible lesson, or some other teaching of God's word.

ADMONITION

Psalm 122: 6

Pray for the peace of Jerusalem: they shall prosper that love thee.

Psalm 136: 1

O give thanks unto the LORD; for he is good: for his mercy endureth for ever.

Psalm 150: 6

6 Let everything that hath breath praise the LORD. Praise ye the LORD.

BLESSING FOR THE RIGHTOUS

Psalm 1: 3

And he shall be like a tree planted by the rivers of water, that bringeth forth his fruit in his season; his leaf also shall not wither; and whatsoever he doeth shall prosper.

PRAISE (ADORATION)

Psalm 8:1

O LORD, our Lord, how excellent is thy name in all the earth!

Psalm 9:1

I will praise thee, O LORD, with my whole heart; I will shew forth all thy marvellous works.

Psalm 18:46

The LORD liveth; and blessed be my rock; and let the God of my salvation be exalted.

Psalm 47:1

O clap your hands, all ye people; shout unto God with the voice of triumph

AID, RELIEF, OR ESCAPE

Psalm 9:9

The LORD also will be a refuge for the oppressed, a refuge in times of trouble.

Psalm 46:1

God is our refuge and strength, a very present help in trouble.

Psalm 121:1-2

1 I will lift up mine eyes unto the hills, from whence cometh my help.

2 My help cometh from the LORD, which made heaven and earth.

DESTINY

Psalm 9:17, 18

17 The wicked shall be turned into hell, and all the nations that forget God. For the needy shall not always be forgotten: the expectation of the poor shall not perish forever.

18 For the needy shall not always be forgotten: the expectation of the poor shall not perish forever.

PURE (WORD)

Psalm 12: 6

The words of the LORD are pure words: as silver tried in a furnace of earth, purified seven times.

ERRONEOUS INFORMATION

Psalm 14: 1

The fool hath said in his heart, **There is no God**. They are corrupt, they have done abominable works, there is none that doeth good.

PERFECTION

Psalm 18:30

As for God, his way is perfect: the word of the LORD is tried: he is a buckler to all those that trust in him.

PRAYER

Psalm 19:14

Let the words of my mouth, and the meditation of my heart, be acceptable in thy sight, O LORD, my strength, and my redeemer.

PROC LAMATION (KNOWING)

Psalm 23: 1

The LORD is my shepherd; I shall not want.

Psalm 23:6

Surely goodness and mercy shall follow me all the days of my life: and I will dwell in the house of the LORD for ever.

Psalm 103:1-5

1 Bless the LORD, O my soul: and all that is within me, bless his holy name.

2 Bless the LORD, O my soul, and forget not all his benefits:

3 Who forgiveth all thine iniquities; who healeth all thy diseases;

4 Who redeemeth thy life from destruction; who crowneth thee with lovingkindness and tender mercies;

5 Who satisfieth thy mouth with good things; so that thy youth is renewed like the eagle's.

Psalm 118:17

I shall not die, but live, and declare the works of the LORD.

CONFIDENCE

Psalm 27: 1-3

1 The LORD is my light and my salvation; whom shall I fear? the LORD is the strength of my life; of whom shall I be afraid?

2 When the wicked, even mine enemies and my foes, came upon me to eat up my flesh, they stumbled and fell.

3 Though an host should encamp against me, my heart shall not fear: though war should rise against me, in this will I be confident.

Psalm 27:13, 14

13 I had fainted, unless I had believed to see the goodness of the LORD in the land of the living.

14 Wait on the LORD: be of good courage, and he shall strengthen thine heart: wait, I say, on the LORD.

Psalm 55:22

22 Cast thy burden upon the LORD, and he shall sustain thee: he shall never suffer the righteous to be moved

Psalm 63:1-7

1 O God, thou art my God; early will I seek thee: my soul thirsteth for thee, my flesh longeth for thee in a dry and thirsty land, where no water is;

2 To see thy power and thy glory, so as I have seen thee in the sanctuary.

3 Because thy lovingkindness is better than life, my lips shall praise thee.

4 Thus will I bless thee while I live: I will lift up my hands in thy name.

5 My soul shall be satisfied as with marrow and fatness; and my mouth shall praise thee with joyful lips:

6 When I remember thee upon my bed, and meditate on thee in the night watches.

7 Because thou hast been my help, therefore in the shadow of thy wings will I rejoice.

Psalm 119:160

Thy word is true from the beginning: and every one of thy righteous judgments endureth for ever.

DELIVERANCE

Psalm 34: 1-3

1 I will bless the LORD at all times: his praise shall continually be in my mouth.

2 My soul shall make her boast in the LORD: the humble shall hear thereof, and be glad.

3 O magnify the LORD with me, and let us exalt his name together.

Psalm 34: 17-19

17 The righteous cry, and the LORD heareth, and delivereth them out of all their troubles.

18 The LORD is nigh unto them that are of a broken heart; and saveth such as be of a contrite spirit.

19 Many are the afflictions of the righteous: but the LORD delivereth him out of them all.

Psalm 40:1-3

1 I waited patiently for the LORD; and he inclined unto me, and heard my cry.

2 He brought me up also out of an horrible pit, out of the miry clay, and set my feet upon a rock, and established my goings.

3 And he hath put a new song in my mouth, even praise unto our God: many shall see it, and fear, and shall trust in the LORD.

Psalm 72:12

For he shall deliver the needy when he crieth; the poor also, and him that hath no helper.

COMMANDS

Psalm 37:1-11

1 Fret not thyself because of evildoers, neither be thou envious against the workers of iniquity.

2 For they shall soon be cut down like the grass, and wither as the green herb.

3 Trust in the LORD, and do good; so shalt thou dwell in the land, and verily thou shalt be fed.

4 Delight thyself also in the LORD: and he shall give thee the desires of thine heart.

5 Commit thy way unto the LORD; trust also in him; and he shall bring it to pass.

6 And he shall bring forth thy righteousness as the light, and thy judgment as the noonday.

7 Rest in the LORD, and wait patiently for him: fret not thyself because of him who prospereth in his way, because of the man who bringeth wicked devices to pass.

8 Cease from anger, and forsake wrath: fret not thyself in any wise to do evil.

9 For evildoers shall be cut off: but those that wait upon the LORD, they shall inherit the earth.

10 For yet a little while, and the wicked shall not be: yea, thou shalt diligently consider his place, and it shall not be.

11 But the meek shall inherit the earth; and shall delight themselves in the abundance of peace.

Psalm 46:10

Be still, and know that I am God: I will be exalted among the heathen, I will be exalted in the earth.

Psalm 49:1-3

1 Hear this, all ye people; give ear, all ye inhabitants of the world:

2 Both low and high, rich and poor, together.

3 My mouth shall speak of wisdom; and the meditation of my heart shall be of understanding.

DIRECTION

Psalm 119: 105

Thy word is a lamp unto my feet, and a light unto my path.

Psalm 37: 23-25

23 The steps of a good man are ordered by the LORD: and he delighteth in his way.

24 Though he fall, he shall not be utterly cast down: for the LORD upholdeth him with his hand.

25 I have been young, and now am old; yet have I not seen the righteous forsaken, nor his seed begging bread.

RESPONSIBILITY

<u>Psalm 40:9-10</u>

9 I have preached righteousness in the great congregation: lo, I have not refrained my lips, O LORD, thou knowest.

10 I have not hid thy righteousness within my heart; I have declared thy faithfulness and thy salvation: I have not concealed thy *<u>lovingkindnes</u>*s and thy truth from the great congregation. (*<u>Christ)</u>*

APPETITE

<u>Psalm 42:1-2</u>

1 As the hart panteth after the water brooks, so panteth my soul after thee, O God.

2 My soul thirsteth for God, for the living God: when shall I come and appear before God?

FAVOR

Psalm 44:1-3

1 We have heard with our ears, O God, our fathers have told us, what work thou didst in their days, in the times of old.

2 How thou didst drive out the heathen with thy hand, and plantedst them; how thou didst afflict the people, and cast them out.

3 For they got not the land in possession by their own sword, neither did their own arm save them: but thy right hand, and thine arm, and the light of thy countenance, because thou hadst a favour unto them.

Psalm 75:6-7

6 For promotion cometh neither from the east, nor from the west, nor from the south.

7 But God is the judge: he putteth down one, and setteth up another.

PROVIDENCE

Psalm 145: 14-21

14 The LORD upholdeth all that fall, and raiseth up all those that be bowed down.

15 The eyes of all wait upon thee; and thou givest them their meat in due season.

16 Thou openest thine hand, and satisfiest the desire of every living thing.

17 The LORD is righteous in all his ways, and holy in all his works.

18 The LORD is nigh unto all them that call upon him, to all that call upon him in truth.

19 He will fulfil the desire of them that fear him: he also will hear their cry, and will save them.

20 The LORD preserveth all them that love him: but all the wicked will he destroy.

21 My mouth shall speak the praise of the LORD: and let all flesh bless his holy name for ever and ever.

JUDGMENT

<u>Psalm 50:1-6</u>

1 The mighty God, even the LORD, hath spoken, and called the earth from the rising of the sun unto the going down thereof.

2 Out of Zion, the perfection of beauty, God hath shined.

3 Our God shall come, and shall not keep silence: a fire shall devour before him, and it shall be very tempestuous round about him.

4 He shall call to the heavens from above, and to the earth, that he may judge his people.

5 Gather my saints together unto me; those that have made a covenant with me by sacrifice.

6 And the heavens shall declare his righteousness: for God is judge himself. Selah.

ANSWERED PRAYER (What God does when Man acts)

Psalm 50:14-15

14 Offer unto God thanksgiving; and pay thy vows unto the most High:

15 And call upon me in the day of trouble: I will deliver thee, and thou shalt glorify me.

Psalm 91: 14-16

14 Because he hath set his love upon me, therefore will I deliver him: I will set him on high, because he hath known my name.

15 He shall call upon me, and I will answer him: I will be with him in trouble; I will deliver him, and honour him.

16 With long life will I satisfy him, and shew him my salvation.

FORGIVENESS AND CLEANSING

Psalm 51:1-6

1 Have mercy upon me, O God, according to thy lovingkindness: according unto the multitude of thy tender mercies blot out my transgressions.

2 Wash me throughly from mine iniquity, and cleanse me from my sin.

3 For I acknowledge my transgressions: and my sin is ever before me.

4 Against thee, thee only, have I sinned, and done this evil in thy sight: that thou mightest be justified when thou speakest, and be clear when thou judgest.

5 Behold, I was shapen in iniquity; and in sin did my mother conceive me.

6 Behold, thou desirest truth in the inward parts: and in the hidden part thou shalt make me to know wisdom.

7 Purge me with hyssop, and I shall be clean: wash me, and I shall be whiter than snow.

8 Make me to hear joy and gladness; that the bones which thou hast broken may rejoice.

9 Hide thy face from my sins, and blot out all mine iniquities.

10 Create in me a clean heart, O God; and renew a right spirit within me.

11 Cast me not away from thy presence; and take not thy holy spirit from me.

12 Restore unto me the joy of thy salvation; and uphold me with thy free spirit.

13 Then will I teach transgressors thy ways; and sinners shall be converted unto thee.

Psalm 139: 23-24

23 Search me, O God, and know my heart: try me, and know my thoughts:

24 And see if there be any wicked way in me, and lead me in the way everlasting.

VICTORY

Psalm 68:1

Let God arise, let his enemies be scattered: let them also that hate him flee before him.

Psalm 98:1

O sing unto the LORD a new song; for he hath done marvellous things: his right hand, and his holy arm, hath gotten him the victory.

FAITHFULNESS

Psalm 71:17-19

17 O God, thou hast taught me from my youth: and hitherto have I declared thy wondrous works.

18 Now also when I am old and greyheaded, O God, forsake me not; until I have shewed thy strength unto this generation, and thy power to every one that is to come.

19 Thy righteousness also, O God, is very high, who hast done great things: O God, who is like unto thee!

TRUST

Psalm 84:11-12

11 For the LORD God is a sun and shield: the LORD will give grace and glory: no good thing will he withhold from them that walk uprightly.

12 O LORD of hosts, blessed is the man that trusteth in thee.

GUIDANCE

Psalm 86:11

Teach me thy way, O LORD; I will walk in thy truth: unite my heart to fear thy name.

Psalm 90:12

So teach us to number our days, that we may apply our hearts unto wisdom.

Psalm 119:133

Order my steps in thy word: and let not any iniquity have dominion over me.

SECURITY

Psalm 91:5-7

5 Thou shalt not be afraid for the terror by night; nor for the arrow that flieth by day;

6 Nor for the pestilence that walketh in darkness; nor for the destruction that wasteth at noonday.

7 A thousand shall fall at thy side, and ten thousand at thy right hand; but it shall not come nigh thee.

JOY

Psalm 100

Psalm 100

1 Make a joyful noise unto the LORD, all ye lands.

2 Serve the LORD with gladness: come before his presence with singing.

3 Know ye that the LORD he is God: it is he that hath made us, and not we ourselves; we are his people, and the sheep of his pasture.

4 Enter into his gates with thanksgiving, and into his courts with praise: be thankful unto him, and bless his name.

5 For the LORD is good; his mercy is everlasting; and
his truth endureth to all generations.

Psalm 126: 5

They that sow in tears shall reap in joy.

UNITY

Psalm 133: 1

Behold, how good and how pleasant it is for brethren to dwell together in unity!

A SELECTION OF BIBLE VERSIONS & TRANSLATIONS

21st Century King James Version

American Standard Version

Amplified Bible

Contemporary English Version

Dake Annotated Reference Bible

Darby Translation

English Standard Version

Essential Study Bible

God's Word Translation

Good News Version

Holman Christian Standard Bible (New Testament)

King James Version

Living Bible

The Message Bible

New American Standard

New Century Version

New English Bible

New International Version

New King James Version

New Life Bible

New Living Translation

New Revised Standard Version

Young's Literal Translation

www.ingramcontent.com/pod-product-compliance
Ingram Content Group UK Ltd.
Pitfield, Milton Keynes, MK11 3LW, UK
UKHW041918190726
13854UKWH00003B/1306

9 781105 608551